EASTERN

ROOSTERS

GERALDINE KAYE

The Donkey Christmas

illustrated by
Glenys Ambrus

HODDER AND STOUGHTON
London   Sydney   Auckland   Toronto

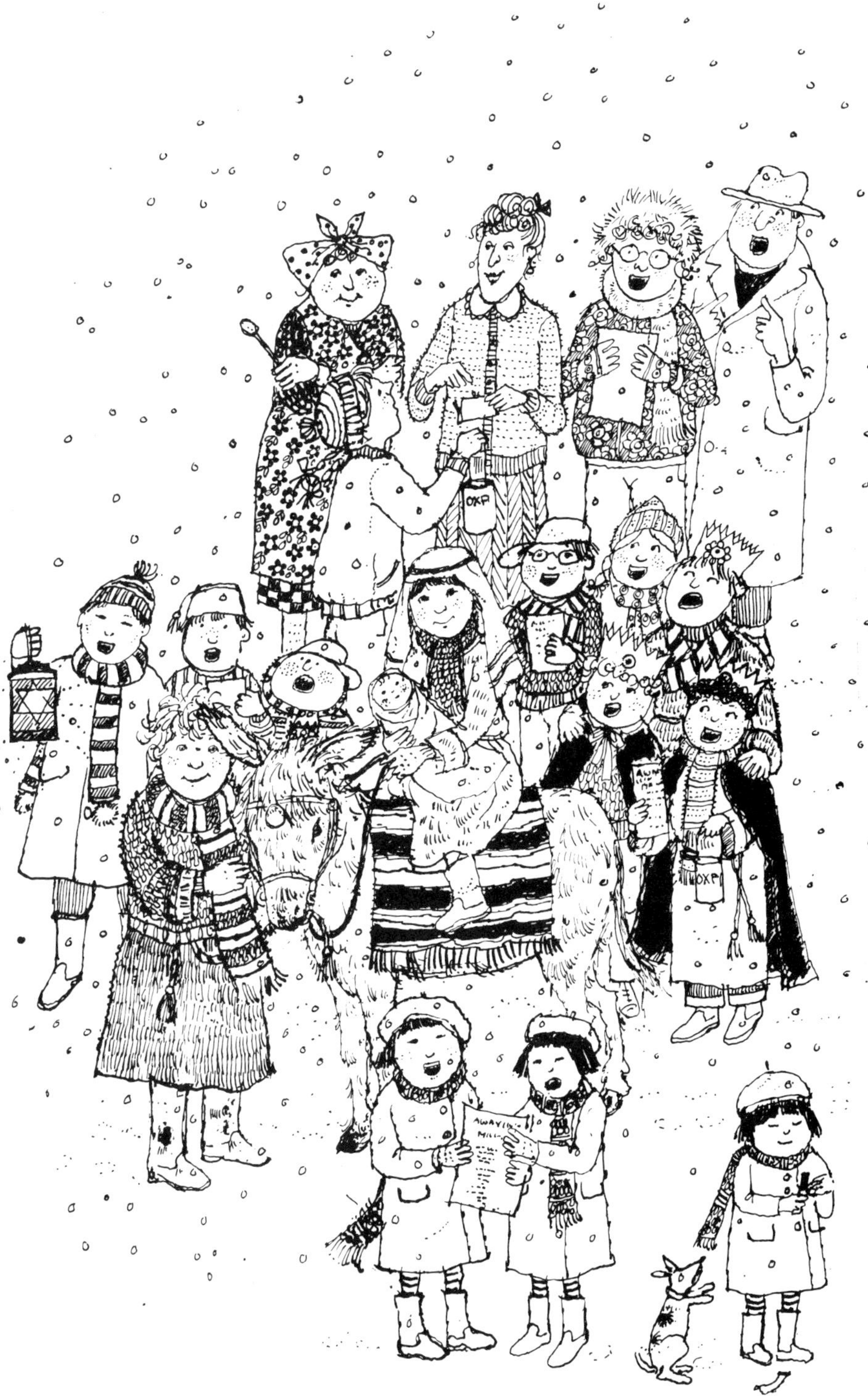

British Library Cataloguing in Publication Data
Kaye, Geraldine *1925–*
 The donkey Christmas.
 I. Title II. Ambrus, Glenys
 823'.914 [J]
 ISBN 0-340-42318-8

Text copyright © Geraldine Kaye 1988
Illustrations copyright © Hodder and Stoughton Ltd 1988

First published 1988

All rights reserved. No part of this publication may be
reproduced or transmitted in any form or by any means,
electronically or mechanically, including photocopying,
recording, or any information storage and retrieval system,
without either the prior permission in writing from the
publisher or a licence permitting restricted copying. In the
United Kingdom such licences are issued by the Copyright
Licensing Agency, 33-34 Alfred Place, London WC1E 7DP.

Published by Hodder and Stoughton Children's Books,
a division of Hodder and Stoughton Ltd,
Mill Road, Dunton Green, Sevenoaks, Kent TN13 2YJ

Photoset in Great Britain by En to En,
Tunbridge Wells, Kent

Printed in Great Britain by T. J. Press (Padstow) Ltd,
Padstow, Cornwall

1 A Real Donkey

It was almost Christmas and Back Lane School was getting ready for the Christmas play.

Lucy was Mary this year and Fitzy and Jake and Daren (who were in Billy's Gang) were the three Kings.

'What can I be?' said Billy.

'You can be the Inn-keeper,' said Miss Lee.

'But the Inn-keeper was rotten,' Billy said. 'I don't want to be the rotten Inn-keeper. Can't I be Joseph?'

'No,' said Miss Lee and that was that.

Billy was fed up.

In the school hall Barry and Garry (who were in the High Street Gang) were getting things ready for the Christmas play.

'What's that?' Billy said.

'It's a cardboard donkey,' Barry said. 'Mary holds it up and it looks like a real donkey.'

'No it doesn't,' Billy said.

'Well, it will when everybody's singing "Oh, little town of Bethlehem",' Barry said.

But Billy had a better idea.

Back in the classroom everybody was talking at once and Miss Lee was saying, 'Listen, Shepherds and Joseph and Innkeeper and Mary, you can all wear your dressing-gowns back-to-front. Have you got a blue dressing-gown, Lucy, and a tea-cloth with a blue band, because Mary should wear blue? Well, don't forget to bring them on Monday for the practice play...'

Billy said, 'That cardboard donkey looks stupid, shall I try and borrow a *real* donkey?'

'Yes, yes, Billy,' said Miss Lee who hadn't really heard because of everybody talking at once. 'Don't forget to bring your dressing-gown on Monday, will you?'

All the way home Billy was working out how he could borrow a *real* donkey for the Christmas play.

Last summer Billy had camped at Beachsea and helped Mr Dodds with his donkeys. The donkeys liked Billy very much and Billy liked the donkeys, especially Misty who was a little grey donkey like a misty day.

When Billy got home he phoned up Beachsea.

Billy said, 'Hello, Mr Dodds. How's Misty?'

Mr Dodds said, 'She's up the big field, same as the others.'

Billy said, 'Can we borrow Misty for our Christmas play?'

Mr Dodds said, 'How you going to get her there?'

Billy said, 'Couldn't you bring her in the horse-box?'

Mr Dodds said, 'No way. You forget the price of petrol. Your dad can fetch her in the van.'

Billy told Dick and Ann and Lucy what Mr Dodds said.

Dick said, 'Get our dad to fetch a donkey in his van, you daft or what?'

Lucy said, 'What do donkeys eat?'

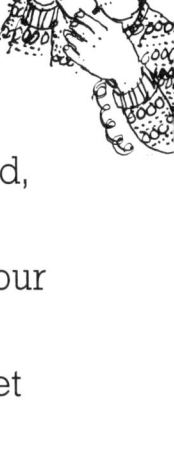

Ann said, 'Where can we put Misty anyway?'

Billy said, 'She can sleep in the kitchen, she's only small.'

Dick said, 'You *are* daft.'

Then Dad came home.

Mum said, 'What time do you call this then? It may be Christmas at the Lamb and Flag but it's not Christmas in this house yet, not by a long chalk, so don't blame me if your tea's gone cold,' and she took Tom and Polly up to bed.

'What's up with her?' Dad said.

Ann said, 'Shall I get you a cup of tea, Dad?'

Billy said, 'Shall I heat up your fish fingers?'

Lucy said, 'Shall I do you an egg instead?'

Dick said, 'Did you have a nice day, Dad?'

'What's up with you lot?' Dad said.

Billy said, 'Well ... Miss Lee wants a real donkey instead of a cardboard donkey for the Christmas play and Mr Dodds says we can borrow Misty if you fetch her in the van.'

Dad said, 'If you think I'm going down to Beachsea fetching donkeys all weekend, you've another think coming.'

But everybody said, 'Oh, please, Dad, she can stop in the shed ... please, Dad ... PLEASE ...'

'Oh, all right,' Dad said. 'As it's Christmas.'

2 Misty

On Saturday morning Dick and Ann took everything out of the shed and Billy took everything out of his money-box and went down Back Lane and all along the High Street to see Miss Cross at the riding school.

Billy said, 'We've got a donkey coming to stay. Can you let us have some hay and stuff?'

Miss Cross said, 'What about my ponies? I'm short of food as it is.'

Billy said, 'Oh, please...'

Miss Cross said, 'Well, just this once... as it's Christmas,' and she gave them hay for food and straw for the donkey's bed.

That night Billy was very excited because having donkeys to stay does get people very excited.

He lay in bed and thought about the donkeys at Beachsea who were Hurry and Curry and Dandy and Mandy and Bingo and Ringo and Ruby and Daisy and Hotdog and Sinbad and Twisty and Misty of course.

And when he went to sleep, he dreamed about Misty.

On Sunday morning Billy and Lucy and Dad set out to Beachsea in the van. When they got there they knocked on the door of Mr Dodds's house, and he came out with a bridle and a bucket of oats.

Then they went up to the big field and there was Misty who had long furry ears and big dark eyes and was grey as a misty day.

Hurry and Curry and Candy and Mandy and Bingo and Ringo and Daisy and Ruby and Hotdog and Sinbad and Twisty were in the big field as well as Misty and that was twelve donkeys. They were all very pleased to see Billy but they hadn't been working since last October and they were a bit frisky. When they saw the bucket of oats, they all got very excited and they all came round and pushed with their noses and the oats got spilt.

But fortunately Billy got the bridle on Misty's head.

Billy was very pleased to see Misty, and Misty was very pleased to see Billy but unfortunately she didn't like the look of the van.

'In you go,' said Mr Dodds but Misty didn't because donkeys never do things unless they want to. Mr Dodds and Dad pushed and Billy pulled but it didn't do any good because Misty stuck her front legs out and pulled and pushed back and, though she was small, she was very strong.

'Full of surprises, this one,' said Mr Dodds. 'Good as gold as a rule.'

Fortunately Billy had got some ginger-nuts in his pocket and Misty liked ginger-nuts better than anything and after that she went in the van.

'You're going to be in the Christmas play,' Billy said.

'Hee-haw,' said Misty.

'Look out, she'll get the picnic basket,' Dad said but fortunately Misty didn't like cheese sandwiches.

It was almost dark when they left Beachsea.

Billy sat in the back of the van and sang 'Oh, little town of Bethlehem' all the way home so Misty would get used to it. Misty was as good as gold.

When they got back to Back Lane, Billy took Misty out to the shed. It looked like a real stable with yellow straw and hay in a box in the corner and Misty went straight in.

'Hee-haw,' said Misty as if she liked it.

But when Billy went inside the house she kicked the door and went on kicking it for a long time.

On Monday at Back Lane School it was *meant* to be lessons in the morning and Christmas-play-practice in the afternoon.

'You know you said a real donkey would be better than a cardboard donkey?' Billy said.

'Did I?' said Miss Lee.

'Yes, and my dad and me went all the way to Beachsea and we borrowed Misty for the play and she's just outside.'

'Oh dear,' said Miss Lee. All Class Three were outside too by this time.

'What's going on?' the Head Teacher said. 'Why is everybody out in the playground when the bell hasn't gone?'

'Er... because we've got a *real* donkey for the Christmas play,' said Miss Lee.

'As long as it knows how to behave,' said the Head Teacher, but he seemed quite pleased.

Mr Grump, the caretaker, wasn't pleased at all. He said, 'I don't get paid for cleaning up after blinking donkeys, and that's a fact.'

3 **The Christmas Play**

So Class Three didn't have lessons on Monday morning after all because they needed extra Christmas-play-practice with a real donkey.

'You'd better bring her inside,' said Miss Lee and Billy led Misty in through the door and all along the passage and into the school hall.

Then everybody put their dressing-gowns on back-to-front and Lucy got on to Misty's back because she was Mary and Billy went into the Inn because he was the Inn-keeper, and Misty tried to go too.

'Stop it,' said Garry because he was Joseph, and he took hold of the bridle and then he said, 'We are going to Bethlehem to pay our taxes.' But Misty stuck out her front legs and wouldn't go to Bethlehem or anywhere else though Garry pushed and pulled and Lucy said, 'Trot on.'

'Oh dear,' said Miss Lee.

'She'll go anywhere with Billy,' Lucy said.

'All right,' said Miss Lee. 'Garry, you had better be the Inn-keeper and let Billy be Joseph.'

'It's not fair, I don't want to be the rotten Inn-keeper,' Garry said, but he went.

After that the practice went quite well.

Joseph said, 'We are going to Bethlehem to pay our taxes,' and he led Misty up and down the stage and her feet went clip-clop. When they got to the stable at the Inn, Misty just stood by the manger, good as gold.

After school Billy took Misty home and her hooves went clip-clop all along the pavement and half of Back Lane School came too.

They said, 'Isn't she sweet?' and, 'You are lucky,' and, 'What dear little feet!' and, 'I wish I had a donkey to stay,' and things like that.

'Hee-haw,' said Misty and she kicked up her heels because a lot of children crowding round made her feel frisky and she went on kicking the shed door for quite a long time and Mrs Twitch came round.

The Christmas play was at three o'clock on Tuesday afternoon and by ten to three everybody was dressed and ready and very excited.

The school hall was rather dark but Billy looked through the curtains and he saw lots of mums and dads and sisters and brothers and aunts and grans sitting in rows. The Head Teacher sat in the front row and the Vicar was next to him.

'Hee-haw,' said Misty and everybody laughed and Billy gave her a ginger-nut to keep her quiet.

'Hush,' said Miss Lee and everybody hushed and the curtains opened and the play began. This time it was the *real* Christmas play and just for a bit Lucy forgot she was Lucy and became Mary and Billy forgot he was Billy and became Joseph. Unfortunately Misty didn't forget she was Misty.

First Mary was sitting on the stage all by herself and then Gabriel came in with big white wings and told her about the baby. While he was talking Joseph gave Misty another ginger-nut biscuit to keep her quiet which it did except for *crunch-munch*.

Then Joseph came out and said, 'Mary, my dear wife, I've got to go to Bethlehem to pay my taxes.'

Mary said, 'I don't fancy being left on my own with a baby coming, I'll get on the donkey and come with you,' and that's what she did. But getting on the donkey's back was a bit difficult because of the dressing-gown back-to-front.

'Off we go to Bethlehem,' Joseph said and he led Mary and the donkey up and down and Misty's hooves went clip-clop on the stage and everybody in Back Lane School sang 'Oh, little town of Bethlehem'.

After a bit Mary started saying, 'How far is it to Bethlehem?' and, 'I'm very tired, Joseph,' and, 'Can't we stop here?' and things like that.

Then Joseph said, 'Never mind, Mary. We will find an inn and you can rest.'

But Misty began to get rather excited.

Then Joseph knocked at the inn door and Misty threw up her heels and kicked the door as well and Joseph said, 'Stop that.' Then he said, 'Can we stay at your inn?'

'Sorry,' said the Inn-keeper, 'no room. We're full right up. Anyway I don't like donkeys.'

'Oh, please,' said Joseph. 'After all it is Christmas.'

The Inn-keeper said, 'Well, you could stop in the stable with the cows if you like.'

'Thanks,' said Joseph, and the curtains closed.

After that the curtains stayed closed and Deng stood on a chair behind them and shone his star and the three Shepherds followed it and so did the three Kings.

Then the curtains opened again and there was Joseph and Mary, and baby Jesus lying on some yellow straw, and Misty and a cardboard cow.

Everybody gasped and said, 'Isn't that lovely?' and Back Lane School sang 'Away in a manger'.

Unfortunately Misty was getting rather excited and Joseph had run out of ginger-nuts.

Misty didn't like the cardboard cow and first she tried to bite it and then she kicked up her heels and knocked it right over.

'Stop it,' said Joseph.

'Oh dear,' said Miss Lee.

Then the three Shepherds came in, and the three Kings with their gifts, and Mary said, 'Stop it,' because Misty was trying to eat the straw in the manger but fortunately Joseph found one more ginger-nut in his dressing-gown pocket, and then everybody sang 'We wish you a Merry Christmas', and the curtains closed and that was the end.

Unfortunately being in Christmas plays does get donkeys very excited and Misty was very excited indeed by this time and she kicked up her heels and knocked over the manger and then she backed against the curtains and the curtains fell down.

'Hee-haw,' said Misty and everybody laughed and clapped.

'Oh dear,' said Miss Lee.

4 Carol Singing

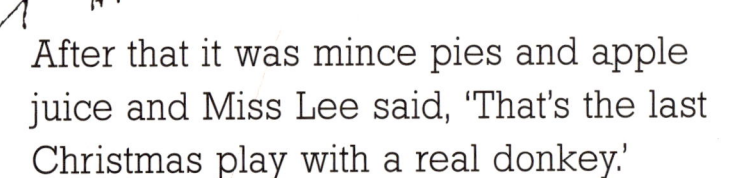

After that it was mince pies and apple juice and Miss Lee said, 'That's the last Christmas play with a real donkey.'

But the Head Teacher said, 'It's the best Christmas play you've done.'

And the Vicar said, 'A real donkey is a very good idea. We're going carol-singing for OXFAM tomorrow night. Could we borrow Joseph and the donkey?'

'Well ... you'll have to ask Billy,' said Miss Lee and Billy said, 'You'll have to ask my dad,' and Dad said, 'All right ... as it's Christmas.'

And Misty ate a mince pie.

Then it was time to go home and Billy led Misty back along the pavement and her hooves went clip-clop and the other half of Back Lane School came too and they said, 'Ooh, it's like a real stable,' and, 'Is that a manger?' and, 'I wish I had a donkey,' and things like that.

Misty got very excited with so many children crowding round and she kicked the door of her shed and went on kicking it for rather a long time.

The next night was carol-singing night.

'Wrap up warm,' Mum said. 'It's really cold. I think it's going to snow.'

Billy put on his dressing-gown back to front and his jersey and scarf over that and the Vicar came and so did Fitzy and Daren and Jake and Deng and Dick and Ann and Lucy and lots of people from Back Lane School.

'We'll go all down Back Lane and along the High Street with Joseph and the donkey out in front,' the Vicar said, and that's what they did and Misty's hooves went clip-clop on the pavement.

They sang 'While shepherds watched' and 'Away in a manger' and then Joseph knocked at the door.

Mrs Twitch said, 'I don't hold with donkeys kicking sheds all night but as it's Christmas . . .' and gave them twenty pence.

It began to snow. Big soft snowflakes floated down in the dark like white feathers.

First Billy's scarf and Misty's rug were spotted with white and soon there was nothing but white as far as you could see and Misty's hooves made no sound at all in the snow.

'A white Christmas is the best sort,' Billy said.

'Thank you for coming but I think you had all better go home now,' the Vicar said and that was what they did.

It snowed all night and in the morning the snow was deep and crisp and even and you could hardly see which backyard was which.

Billy and Lucy dug a path to the shed. It took quite a long time but it didn't matter as it was the first day of the holidays.

Billy gave Misty the rest of the hay and some clean water.

'I'm not taking the van out in this,' said Dad. 'Your donkey'll have to stop where she is.'

'But we're out of hay, we'll have to go back to Miss Cross,' said Billy. And that's what they did.

But Miss Cross said, 'Sorry, I need all the hay I've got for my own ponies, Christmas or no Christmas.'

Fortunately Billy had another idea.

5 A White Christmas

'Why don't we go carol-singing *again* for donkey food?' Billy said and Fitzy and Daren and Jake and Deng and Lucy and Dick and Ann came too and so did Misty. It was very cold and the snow was so crisp that it crunched like sugar under her hooves.

They sang 'Oh, little town of Bethlehem' and 'We wish you a Merry Christmas' and then they knocked on the door.

'Aren't you the same lot as last night?' said Mrs Twitch.

'Yes,' said Billy. 'But that was for OXFAM and now we're singing for food for our donkey.'

'I'm too soft for my own good,' said Mrs Twitch and she gave them a slice of stale bread. Misty ate it straight away.

After that they went all down Back Lane and they got half a packet of cornflakes and two apples and three carrots and half a loaf of brown bread and a large white and then they went home.

That night Billy woke up and looked out of the window. It was white and cold and very quiet and Billy was worried because Misty wasn't kicking the shed door.

'What's up?' said Billy and he crept downstairs in his dressing-gown (right way round), and went out to the shed.

'Misty?' he said.

It was dark in the shed and Billy shone his torch. First he saw yellow straw and then he saw Misty standing in the straw and then he saw something lying in the straw.

It was a baby donkey.

Misty had had a snow-white donkey foal.

Next day Billy phoned Mr Dodds.

Billy said, 'Misty's got a foal. It's white.'

Mr Dodds said, 'Full of surprises, that one.'

Billy said, 'But we can't bring the donkeys back because of the snow.'

Mr Dodds said, 'Don't worry yourself. Just keep her warm and well-fed, long as she's back for Easter.'

'Easter?' said Billy. 'That's all very well. . .'

Lucy wrote S.O.S. FEED OUR DONKEYS in the snow outside and soon everybody in Back Lane wanted to see the donkey foal and nearly everybody brought something for the donkeys, so Misty had plenty to eat after all. The snow stayed for more than a week, and so it was a white Christmas everywhere that year.

But after Christmas the snow went grey and then it began to melt and soon there were just snow islands in a sea of brown mud.

'Looks like we might get down to Beachsea on New Year's Day,' Dad said and that's what they did.

On New Year's Day, Misty and the foal and Billy and Lucy got in the back of the van and Mum and Polly and Tom got in the front and Dad drove everybody down to Beachsea.

'Nice little foal, that is,' said Mr Dodds. 'You did a good job looking after them, Billy.'

'I liked it,' said Billy. 'A white Christmas is nice and a white donkey Christmas is the best Christmas there is.'

'Hee-haw,' said Misty.